The Caregiver's Quiet Strength

A Coloring Book for Caregivers

Honoring the Strength That Lives Beneath the Surface

Dawn Jones

Copyright © 2026 by Dawn Jones
All rights reserved.
No part of this book may be reproduced, distributed, or transmitted in any form or by any means, including photocopying, recording, or other electronic or mechanical methods, without the prior written permission of the publisher, except in the case of brief quotations embodied in reviews and certain other noncommercial uses permitted by copyright law.

This book is a coloring and reflection resource. It is not intended to replace professional medical, psychological, or therapeutic advice. Please consult a qualified professional for specific care needs.

Printed in the United States of America.

Portions of this book were created with the assistance of artificial intelligence as a creative support tool. All final selections, edits, and arrangement were guided and approved by the author.

A Gentle Note for the Caregiver

This book is for the caregiver.

There is no right way to color these pages.

There is no timeline.

There is no expectation.

There is only space to breathe.

Dedication

For caregivers everywhere —
seen and unseen

**For caregivers everywhere —
your strength matters.**

I am rooted, even when life feels uncertain.

I stand firm, even on the days I feel tired.

I am allowed to move slowly and still be strong.

I give myself permission to pause.

My presence matters more than I realize.

I take this journey one step at a time.

I do not have to see the whole path to keep going.

Each day I show up is an act of courage.

I honor how far I have already come.

Even when the road is long, I am not alone.

Rest is not weakness; it is wisdom.

Quiet moments help restore my strength.

Like this plant, I remain strong and healthy through every season.

I am worthy of care, too.

I give myself permission to pause.

It is safe for me to rest when I can.

I breathe in calm and release what I cannot control.

I do not need to be perfect to be enough.

Balance looks different in every season of life.

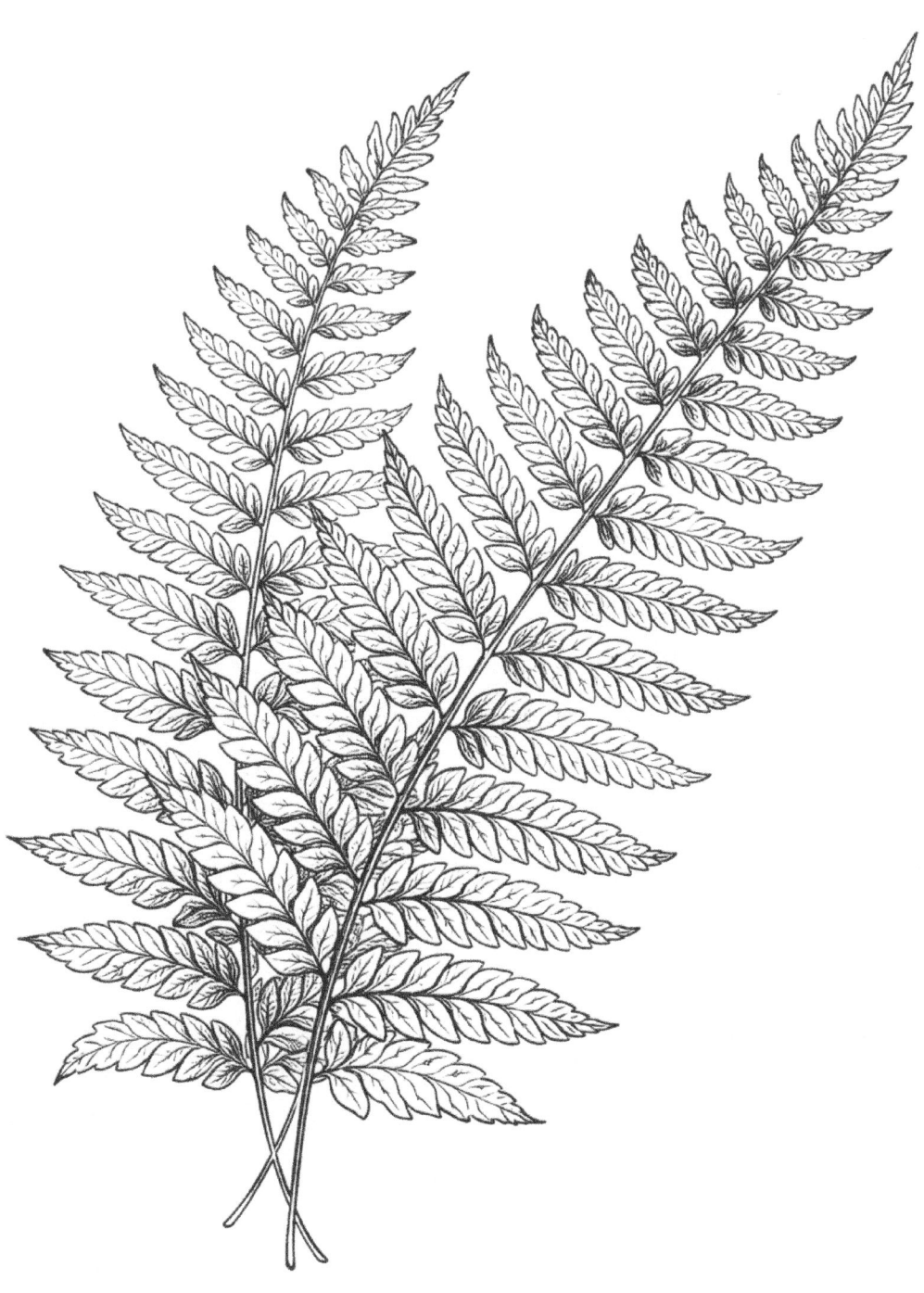

I allow myself grace today.

Peace begins with a single breath.

I am allowed to let go of what no longer serves me.

Even now, I am becoming something new.

My strength may be quiet, but it is real.

I carry love,
even when the work is heavy.

I am stronger than I feel
in this moment.

I am doing the best I can and that is enough.

I choose gentleness for myself today.

Hope can be soft and still be powerful.

I carry quiet strength into tomorrow.

Made in the USA
Coppell, TX
11 February 2026